The Super Soybean

Raymond Bial

Albert Whitman & Company, Morton Grove, Illinois

The Super Soybean is respectfully dedicated to American farmers and their families, who have worked so hard to make a better world for everyone.

Library of Congress Cataloging-in-Publication Data

Bial, Raymond.

The super soybean / by Raymond Bial.

p. cm.

Includes index.

ISBN 10: 0-8075-7549-6 (hardcover) ISBN 13: 978-0-8075-7549-9 (hardcover)

1. Soybean—Juvenile literature. 2. Soybean products—Juvenile literature. I. Title.

SB205.S7B485 2007 633.3'4—dc22 2007014165

The design is by Carol Gildar.

This book has been printed with soybean ink.

For more information about Albert Whitman & Company, please visit our web site at www.albertwhitman.com.

Soybean plants about five weeks old.

Soybeans are one of the most super plants in the world. They are super food. And they can be used for an amazing variety of things—fuel, plastics, soap, and medicines. Even the ink in this book—used to print the words and the photographs—is made from soybeans!

Most soybeans are used to feed animals—chickens, pigs, and cows. Soybeans are used in cat and dog foods, and to feed fish raised on fish farms.

In many Asian countries, people have been eating soybeans for thousands of years. More and more, Americans are eating soybeans, too. Soybeans provide protein, like meat or eggs do, and contain many vitamins, minerals, and other healthy ingredients. They have little fat.

We eat soybean curd known as tofu. Roasted soybeans make a good snack, as does edamame, soybeans boiled in their green pods and served with salt. A chunky, tender cake of whole fermented soybeans called tempeh makes a good substitute for meat. Soybeans are sold canned and frozen. We like to season our food with soy sauce. (The word soy comes from the Japanese word shoyu, which means "sauce.")

Soybean flakes are crushed to squeeze out oil, which is low in saturated fats and high in healthy omega-3 fatty acids. It is used in cooking oils, salad

American livestock devour 33.4 million tons of soybean meal every year.

Soybeans can be used to make hot dogs!

oils, shortening, margarine, and mayonnaise. It can even be processed into a spread called soy butter. Soybean oil now makes up more than a third of all the vegetable fats and oils consumed by Americans.

Soy flour is like the flour of wheat and other grains, but it is especially high in protein. Soy flour is used for many kinds of pasta and baked goods, including breads, cookies, cakes, and snacks.

Soy flour is used to make textured vegetable protein, or TVP, which comes in many shapes—flakes, chunks, and flat pieces. TVP can replace meat entirely (for example, in vegetarian burgers and hot dogs) or partly replace it in foods like sausages and chili.

Providing people and animals with protein from soybeans is also cheaper than providing protein from meat.

It's fun to eat edamame.

Soybeans are super-easy to grow. The plants grow quickly—it takes about four months from planting to harvest. And they don't need much fertilizer. This is because the soybean is a legume. Other legumes are peanuts, peas, beans, lentils, and clover.

Legumes have small growths, or nodules, on their roots. Rhizobia bacteria in these nodules take nitrogen from the air in the soil. Both the bacteria and the soybean plant use this nitrogen to thrive, and eventually, the nitrogen is released back into the soil to make it more fertile. Farmers often plant soybeans one year and another crop, like corn, in the same field the next year because the soybean crop has improved the soil.

Soybeans do need warm weather and the right amount of moisture. In the four months or so from planting to harvesting, soybeans grow best with rainfall of at least eight to ten inches. Soybeans also require average daily temperatures between seventy and eighty degrees Fahrenheit (twenty-one and twenty-six degrees centigrade). The number of long warm days, known as "the growing season," affects the flowering and ripening of soybeans and the kinds that are planted.

In the southern United States, where the weather is very warm, soybeans are planted from early spring to midsummer, and they are sometimes planted again late in the summer, to be harvested late in the fall.

Most soybeans are grown in the Midwest, where vast stretches of land are fertile and the summers are hot and humid. There are many soybean fields in Ohio, Michigan, Indiana, Illinois, Iowa, Missouri, Nebraska, Wisconsin, Minnesota, North Dakota, and South Dakota. The most are grown in Illinois and Iowa. In the United States, more than 75 million acres of soybeans are planted every year.

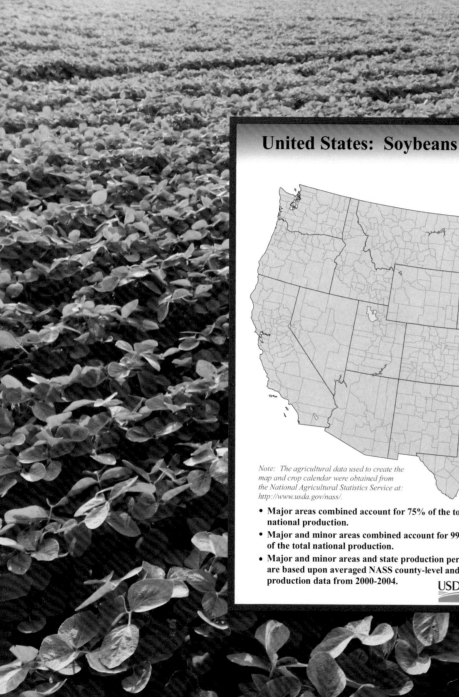

United States: Soybeans

Yellow numbers indicate the percent each state contributed to the total national production. States not numbered contributed less than 1% to the national total.

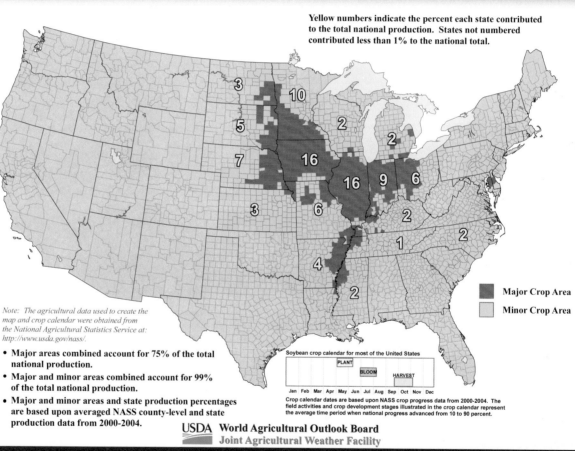

Major Crop Area

Minor Crop Area

Note: The agricultural data used to create the map and crop calendar were obtained from the National Agricultural Statistics Service at: http://www.usda.gov/nass/.

- Major areas combined account for 75% of the total national production.
- Major and minor areas combined account for 99% of the total national production.
- Major and minor areas and state production percentages are based upon averaged NASS county-level and state production data from 2000-2004.

Soybean crop calendar for most of the United States

PLANT
BLOOM
HARVEST

Jan Feb Mar Apr May Jun Jul Aug Sep Oct Nov Dec

Crop calendar dates are based upon NASS crop progress data from 2000-2004. The field activities and crop development stages illustrated in the crop calendar represent the average time period when national progress advanced from 10 to 90 percent.

USDA **World Agricultural Outlook Board**
Joint Agricultural Weather Facility

In the Midwest, the fields are frozen or covered with a blanket of snow throughout the long winter. Come spring, the days lengthen, the air warms, and the soil gradually softens. The fields are usually ready for planting from about mid-May to early June, when the soil temperature is at least fifty-five to sixty degrees Fahrenheit (thirteen to sixteen degrees centigrade).

Seed beans are poured into the planter.

Soybeans are planted with a special "planter," which is pulled behind a tractor. The planter digs long rows or troughs, about one to one and one-half inches deep and about thirty inches apart. The planter then drops seed beans one at a time about two inches apart and covers them with a layer of soil.

The planter digs the rows, drops in the seeds, and covers them with soil.

Four to seven days after planting, the soybean seed grows a little tail-like root called a radicle. This becomes the main root, or taproot. Soon many other lateral, or sideways, hairlike roots spread out from it. The taproot can reach depths of four to eight feet in some soils, but it is usually about two feet long. Most of the lateral roots are in the upper six to twelve inches of soil. At the same time the radicle starts to grow, the cotyledon (KAHT uh LEE duhn), a stem and little round leaf, pops through the ground. Then groups of three, or trifoliate (TRY FOH lee uht), leaves open up.

By early June, tiny soybean plants have sprouted from the nutrient-rich black soil, and the crop is on its way.

Through the hot summer, soybean plants may shoot up as much as an inch a day. In a few weeks, the bushy green soybeans may be a foot tall, and before long they will be knee-high or even taller. Very small white or purple flowers appear on the plants by mid- to late summer.

Soybeans may grow to be from one to six feet tall. The kinds planted in the United States grow to about three feet tall.

Soybean leaves are trifoliate, which means they are in groups of three.

Soybean leaves are very small, about one-fourth inch high.

Small growths or nodules on the roots contain rhizobia bacteria.

11

Fine hairs cover the soybean pods.

Over the coming weeks, the tiny flowers form small pods of soybeans. Each plant may have sixty to eighty pods. By early autumn, the stems, leaves, and pods become covered with brown or gray hair.

Inside the pods are two, three, and occasionally four beans. Soybeans vary strikingly in color: blond, greenish yellow, green, brown, or black.

Soybeans ready to harvest.

Some are so pale that people call them "white," though there are no truly white soybeans. Soybeans can be two-colored, usually green or yellow with a saddlelike black or brown patch on each side. And some soybeans are brindled, meaning they are striped or spotted brown and black.

All soybeans have a spot called a hilum, which is black, brown, gray, buff, or yellow. The hilum is a scar left from the place the bean was attached to the pod.

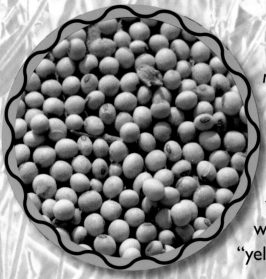

The scientific name of the soybean grown today is *Glycine max.* The soybean probably originated from a wild Asian plant known as *Glycine ussuriensis,* which did not grow upright but along the ground. There is a record of the Chinese growing soybeans for food in the eleventh century B.C.E.—more than three thousand years ago. Soybeans were considered one of the five sacred grains essential to Chinese civilization, along with rice, wheat, barley, and millet. They were also known as the "yellow jewel."

By 712 C.E., the soybean had made its way to Japan. It was not until the sixteenth and seventeenth centuries that Europeans began visiting China and Japan and learned about soybeans. In 1740, the soybean was grown in gardens in France and in 1790 in the Royal Botanic Garden in England, but only as a curiosity.

In 1765, Samuel Bowen introduced soybeans to North America. He brought soybeans from China to London and then to Savannah, Georgia. He grew the soybeans on his plantation and made soy sauce and vermicelli, or thin noodles, for export to England. In 1769, Bowen sent a sample of "Chinese vetches," or soybeans, to the American Philosophical Society in Philadelphia. In 1770, Benjamin Franklin sent soybean seeds from London to botanist John Bartram in Philadelphia. But it is not known if any soybeans were grown at that time in the Philadelphia area, and when Bowen died in 1777, his soybean venture ended.

By 1804, James Mease, a physician and amateur horticulturist, reported, "The soybean is adapted to Pennsylvania, and should be cultivated." In 1829, Professor Thomas Nuttall also reported that soybeans thrived in the botanic garden in Cambridge, Massachusetts. Other early scientists were beginning to experiment with soybeans, too.

Soybean plants about ninety days old.

During the Civil War (1861-1865), soybeans were sometimes used as "coffee berries" to brew a hot drink for soldiers because coffee beans were scarce. Yet farmers did not begin to grow a lot of soybeans until the late 1800s.

In the 1890s, scientists in the United States began to test soybeans as food for animals. In 1898, the United States Department of Agriculture (USDA) introduced several varieties from Asian countries and set up a system to keep track of different kinds of seed.

George Washington Carver working in his laboratory.

In 1904, George Washington Carver began studying soybeans at the Tuskegee Institute in Alabama. Although he is best known for his work with peanuts, Carver discovered a method of extracting soybean oil and found many ways to use it. He later invented a process for making paints and stains from soybeans. Most importantly, he encouraged farmers in the South to plant soybeans, along with peanuts and other legumes, to help keep the soil fertile so that cotton and other important crops could be successful.

Most farmers still ignored soybeans, but that was about to change. In 1907, William J. "Bill" Morse joined the United States Department of Agriculture, where he studied soybeans as an assistant to Dr. Charles V. Piper. Morse devoted his life to studying soybeans. He was a founder of the American Soybean Association. He wrote more than eighty publications about soybeans, including *The Soybean*, published in 1923, written together with Charles Piper.

At this time, there were about twenty different varieties of soybeans in the United States. From August 1924 through December 1926, Palemon Howard (P. H.) Dorsett collected soybeans in China and sent back fifteen hundred different varieties. In 1929, Dorsett went on another trip, this time with William Morse. When Dorsett became ill, Morse traveled on, in northeast China and Korea. From this expedition about forty-five hundred different kinds of soybeans were sent back to the United States.

Helped by the work of Morse and Dorsett, by the mid-1930s, the USDA had developed many improved varieties. Now farmers became more enthusiastic about growing soybeans. In 1924, about 5 million bushels of soybeans had been produced in the United States. By 1940, the yearly crop had increased to 78 million bushels.

Dorsett (second from the right) and Peter Liu, his Chinese interpreter, traveling to find soybeans.

All the soybeans in the United States come from seeds that have been carefully bred to ensure disease-resistant plants and big harvests. Today, more than 80 percent of soybeans have been genetically modified. This means the basic structure of the plant—the way its cells are formed—has been changed. Plants from such seeds can survive when the fields are sprayed with herbicides. Because farmers are planting the best seeds and using the most modern equipment to cultivate and harvest, the United States now produces the most soybeans in the world—three billion bushels a year.

More than half of these soybeans are exported to markets in Mexico, Europe, and Asia. China, where soybeans originated, now imports them from the United States and Brazil.

China grows its own soybeans, too. Worldwide, the biggest producers of soybeans are the United States, Brazil, Argentina, China, and India. Paraguay, Canada, Bolivia, and Italy are also major soybean producers.

Seed beans treated with fungicides are pink, as shown here.

Soybeans are not hard to grow, but farmers must still carefully tend to their fields. Until recently, weeds had to be yanked out by hand. Everyone in the family might "walk the beans," pulling weeds, row after row, day after day. Today, farmers cultivate their soybeans with a cultivator, a chisel-tooth implement pulled behind a tractor. The hooked blades of the cultivator scrape under the weeds between several rows at a time. Farmers usually cultivate their fields twice a season when the weeds are young and not yet deeply rooted. Once the soybeans are about thirty inches tall, they shade out most weeds. Farmers also fight weeds with herbicides.

The soybean cultivator digs out the weeds.

Adult Japanese beetle feeding on a soybean leaf.

Soybean aphids and ant on a soybean stem. The aphids leave sticky stuff called honeydew, which ants (and ladybugs) feed on.

Soybeans can be damaged by worms and insects, including the soybean aphid, the cutworm, the roundworm, the armyworm, the corn earworm, the green clover worm, the fall armyworm, the soybean leafminer, the velvet bean caterpillar, the stinkbug, the grasshopper, the bean leaf beetle, the blister beetle, the Japanese beetle, and the Mexican bean beetle! Pesticides are often used to protect crops from these enemies.

Soybeans can get many diseases: stem canker, brown stem rot, bacterial leaf diseases, frogeye, target spot, purple seed stain, root rot, and various kinds of fungi. A fungus called soybean rust, or Asian soybean rust, has damaged crops across Asia, Australia, Africa, South America, and recently the United States. Spread by spores, which are blown by the wind, soybean rust was probably carried from Colombia to the southern United States by Hurricane Ivan, the strongest hurricane of 2004.

Scientists did not think that soybean rust would survive the cold winters of the Midwest, but in recent years some has been found there. Farmers hope to control it with fungicide.

Adult bean leaf beetle feeding on a soybean pod.

A crop duster sprays pesticide on a soybean field near Sheldon, Illinois.

Herbicides, pesticides, and fungicides are powerful chemicals that can damage the environment and present health hazards. Research is being done to find the safest chemicals and develop even more "super" soybeans that will stand up to diseases and pests. Some farmers specialize in growing only organic soybeans—soybeans that have been raised without chemical fertilizers, herbicides, pesticides, or fungicides.

Farmers always have to deal with weather problems. It can be too warm or too cool, with too much or too little rain for the crop to thrive.

But if all goes well, by mid-August, soybeans in Illinois stand three feet tall. In the cool of early autumn, the soybeans ripen. The bushy plants fade from lush green to soft yellow, russet, and brown. The leaves flutter like confetti in the wind; many fall off and blow away. The seedpods dangle from the stems, and the soybeans inside become hard and dry. It is time to "bring in the beans."

For harvesting, farmers want clear blue skies. If it rains, the fields may become so soft that the heavy equipment will bog down. The soybeans must also "dry down," until the moisture content is about 13 percent. If the beans are too wet, they will have to be dried with fans that circulate air through the storage bins. This adds extra expense.

At harvest, farmers bring out large machines called combines. Steadily rumbling over the fields, the combines easily harvest several rows in each pass. These complicated machines pick and shell the soybeans. The crushed pods, stems, and leaves fly from the back of the combine and scatter to the ground.

The harvested soybeans are collected in a bin mounted atop the combine. When this bin is full, the farmer pulls the combine alongside a truck or wagon parked on a nearby road shoulder. The soybeans flow through a chute into the vehicle. Once the truck or wagon is filled, the heaping load of soybeans is driven to a local grain elevator, and the combine returns to the field to again chug its way up and down the long rows.

Soybeans flow from the combine into a truck that will be driven to a grain elevator.

Newly harvested soybeans on the top of a combine.

To bring in their soybeans, farmers must work long days, often late into the night. Even in the dark, the combines clatter their way back and forth across the field because no one ever knows how long the weather will hold. If it doesn't rain too much, the harvest usually takes just a few weeks.

One load of soybeans after another is hauled to grain elevators, whose tall concrete storage cylinders rise up into the sky. These towering structures are so prominent on the flat land that they have been called "prairie skyscrapers" and "cathedrals of the prairie."

Truckloads of soybeans are delivered to a grain elevator.

A worker holds a sample of soybeans to be tested for moisture content.

Before the soybeans are unloaded at the elevator, each truck or wagon is weighed along with its load of soybeans. A moisture sample is also taken. The weight of the truck or wagon is subtracted from that of the total load.

The farmer will be paid for his soybeans based on the total weight delivered to the elevator through the harvest season. The price of the soybeans is determined by the market price (what customers are willing to pay for the beans) minus the fees for handling and storage at the grain elevator.

After the soybeans are weighed, they are driven up to the elevator and poured into a "hopper," an underground storage bin covered by a metal grate. From there, spiral-shaped devices called augers in long pipes move a stream of beans into the storage cylinder. Elevator workers must be very careful about grain dust, which is as explosive as flammable gas. People must not smoke or have any kind of flame near the soybeans. Workers stand by to sweep up loose soybeans scattered around the grate.

Soybeans pour from the back of a truck into the hopper, located underground and covered by a metal grate.

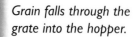
Grain falls through the grate into the hopper.

While the soybeans are in the elevator, moisture and temperature samples are taken frequently. The crop must be kept dry and at just the right temperature or it can develop mold and rot. The best moisture content is between 12 and 14 percent.

Grain elevators are located along railroad tracks so trains can deliver soybeans throughout the country to large processing companies such as Archer-Daniels-Midland, headquartered in Decatur, Illinois. So many soybeans are processed in Decatur the town is known as "Soy City."

From other farming areas in the Midwest, huge loads are shipped by barge down the Mississippi, Ohio, and Missouri rivers to New Orleans. There, soybeans are exported to countries throughout the world.

Soybeans are used not only as food, but also in many products, including plastics. Automaker Henry Ford recognized the amazing possibilities of soybeans. One day in the 1930s, he dumped soybeans on the floor of his research lab and told the scientists, "You guys are supposed to be smart. You ought to be able to do something with them." And the scientists did.

Ford researchers were soon using soybeans to make much of the plastic on cars: gearshift knobs, horn buttons, window frames, accelerator pedals, light-switch assemblies, and ignition-coil casings. On August 13, 1941, Ford unveiled a "Soybean Car." With a frame of tubular steel, this unique car had a body made up of fourteen panels of soybean plastic. It weighed just two thousand pounds—a thousand pounds less than a steel car.

To demonstrate the toughness of the plastic, Ford once hit the trunk of this car with an axe in front of photographers. The Soybean Car was never mass-produced, but today many cars have parts of soybean plastics.

Henry Ford hitting the "Soybean Car."

Soybeans are even used in makeup!

Soy-based plastics are more environmentally friendly than plastics made from petroleum. Unlike petroleum, soybeans are a renewable resource. Once oil is pumped out of the ground and used up, it is gone forever, but another crop of soybeans can be grown every year. Soy plastics are also biodegradable, so they may be safely recycled. Today, soybean products range from toys to tools, along with building materials and garden supplies. Soybeans are used to make many disposable items: plastic utensils (spoons, forks, and knives), plates, trays, and fast-food containers.

Soybeans are used to make soaps that are strong enough to clean graffiti from walls. They can be made into building materials that look just like wood. Soybeans are used in candles, waxes, paints, stains, enamels, adhesives, fire foam stabilizers, varnishes, linoleum, cleaning compounds, disinfectants, textile fibers, medicines, and makeup.

Since you were very young, you have probably enjoyed one soybean product—crayons! Soybeans can be manufactured into crayons that not only cost less than wax crayons, but also have brighter colors. Just one bushel of soybeans can make more than two thousand crayons.

One of the most common uses of soybeans is for printing ink. The manufacture of soy ink releases fewer chemicals into the atmosphere than petroleum-based ink, and it is much easier to recycle paper printed with soy ink. More than eighty thousand newspapers in the United States now use soy inks. Many magazines, books, and other publications are printed with brilliant soy inks.

Like corn ethanol, soy biodiesel is an excellent alternative to petroleum fuel. Soybeans can be used as fuel for automobiles, trucks, and buses. Just one bushel of soybeans yields about 1.5 gallons of biodiesel fuel. Soy biodiesel produces less pollution from exhaust than fossil fuels, both gasoline and diesel. Biodiesel is renewable, and it reduces dependence on oil from other countries.

In recent years, soy biodiesel has become more affordable and available nationwide. Many farmers now power their tractors with this fuel; many cities use soy biodiesel in their buses. Corporations and government agencies use this fuel in their fleets of cars and trucks. Some people even use soy biodiesel in their powerboats. Parks and school districts are increasingly using this fuel in their vehicles. Maybe your school bus uses soy biodiesel!

35

The harvest ends quickly. Combines, tractors, and trucks are pulled into sheds for the winter. If soybean prices are good, farmers can pay for their land and equipment, and earn a profit.

They can begin to plan for the next season.

They are proud of their super soybeans!

Index

Boldface page numbers indicate photographs or illustrations.

Acknowledgments

This book would not have been possible without the help of many individuals and organizations. I would like to thank Kevin Daugherty and the staff of the Illinois Farm Bureau's Ag in the Classroom program, including Ken Kashian, who made several fine photographs available for the book. I would also like to thank the following Illinois grain elevators where I was allowed to make photographs: Anderson's, Champaign; Fisher Farmer's Grain and Coal, Thomasboro; and Grand Prairie Co-op, Philo. I would like to express my appreciation to the many farmers who provided valuable information or allowed me to photograph them at work in the fields, including Dave and Jane Berbaum, Elaine and Max Hershbarger, Lyman Gene and Joan Neef, and Virlon Suits.

John Seder provided wonderful photographs of Ashtyn Jade Seder, Edge Rife, and Kaitlyn Wilebski. A number of organizations also provided photographs for the book, including the Henry Ford Museum, the National Renewable Energy Laboratory (NREL), Nebraska Soybean Association, the New York Public Library, and the United States Department of Agriculture (USDA) Photography Center.

I would especially like to thank my editor, Kathy Tucker, and book designer, Carol Gildar.

Bibliography

A number of books were consulted in the preparation of *The Super Soybean,* notably the following:

Boerma, H. Roger, and James Eugene Specht. *Soybeans: Improvement, Production, and Uses.* Madison, Wisc.: American Society of Agronomy, Crop Science Society of America, Soil Science Society of America, 2004.

Hoeft, Robert G., Samuel R. Aldrich, Emerson D. Nafziger and others. *Modern Corn and Soybean Production.* Champaign, Ill.: MCSP Publications, 2000.

Kenworthy, Leonard Stout. *Soybeans: The Wonder Beans.* New York: Messner, 1976.

Liu, KeShun. *Soybeans: Chemistry, Technology, and Utilization.* New York: Chapman & Hall, 1997.

Additional photo credits: *Page 4:* cattle feeding, United States Soybean Board/Soybean Checkoff. *Page 5:* girl eating soy hotdog, boy and girl eating edamame © John Seder. *Page 7:* map of soybean production in United States, United States Department of Agriculture (USDA). *Page 11:* soybean flower, USDA; soybean illustration from THE WORLD BOOK ENCYCLOPEDIA. © 2007 World Book, Inc. By permission of the publisher. www.worldbook.com. *Page 12:* soybeans ready to harvest, USDA. *Page 13:* open soybean pod; various kinds of soybeans, USDA. *Page 16:* George Washington Carver. Courtesy of the New York Public Library. *Page 17:* Dorsett and Liu on the trail, Special Collections, National Agricultural Library, USDA. *Page 19:* soybean cultivator, USDA. *Page 20:* Japanese beetle, Philip L. Nixon, University of Illinois; soybean aphids © Marlin Rice; bean leaf beetle, University of Illinois Extension. *Page 21:* crop duster, Ken Hammond, Agricultural Research Service, USDA. *Page 33:* Ford hitting soybean car, Henry Ford Museum. *Page 34:* girls with makeup, Ken Kashian, Illinois Farm Bureau. *Pages 34-35:* soybean crayons, Ken Kashian, Illinois Farm Bureau. *Page 35:* soybean bus, Department of Energy (DOE), National Renewable Energy Laboratory (NREL), Nebraska Soybean Association. *Page 37:* Farmer in field, Ken Kashian, Illinois Farm Bureau; hands with soybeans, Ken Kashian, Illinois Farm Bureau.

About the Author

Raymond Bial (pronounced beel) is the author and photo-illustrator of more than ninety critically acclaimed books for children and adults, including *Amish Home; Frontier Home; The Underground Railroad; Where Lincoln Walked; One-Room School; Ghost Towns of the American West; Tenement: Immigrant Life on the Lower East Side; Nauvoo: Mormon City on the Mississippi River;* and twenty-eight titles in "Lifeways," a series of books about Native American Peoples. A skilled photographer, he works with ease in color and black and white, using both film cameras and digital equipment. The subjects of Raymond's books range from farm life to American social and cultural history. He is best known for his versatility in portraiture, landscapes, and still lifes, and his sensitivity toward the people, places, and objects portrayed in his images.

He has also written mystery fiction for children: *The Fresh Grave and Other Ghostly Stories, The Ghost of Honeymoon Creek,* and *Shadow Island: A Tale of Lake Superior.*

Raymond Bial's books have received numerous awards from the American Library Association, the National Council of Teachers of English, the Children's Book Council, and many other organizations. He lives with his wife, Linda, and children Sarah and Luke in Urbana, Illinois. His daughter Anna, who illustrated two of Raymond's books, is a fashion designer in New York City.